BEFORE FEDEX, THERE WAS THE PONY EXPRESS

History Book 3rd Grade

Children's History

The lone rider speeds across the prairie, urging his horse along. He has to go fast because the news won't wait, never mind the danger! Read on and learn about the short, exciting life of the Pony Express.

THE NEED FOR NEWS

In the middle of the nineteenth century, the United States was growing. There were big cities and states on the east coast, and California was booming on the west coast.

PONY EXPRESS TRAIL
1860-1861

Sioux Indians in the Mountains

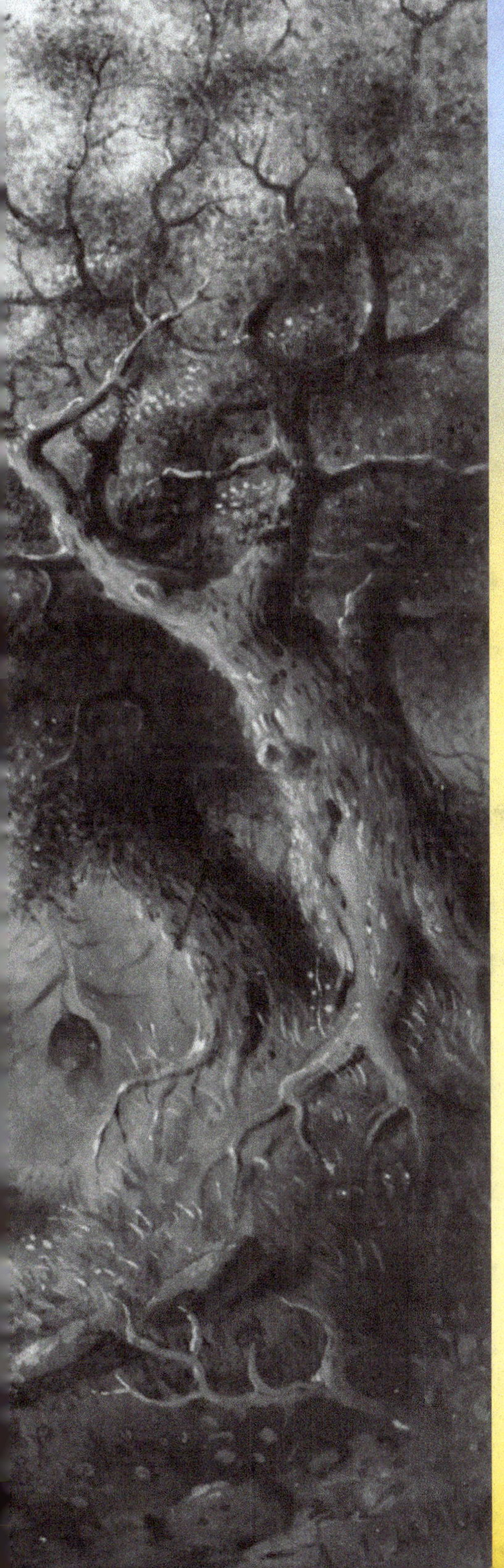

The middle of the country was not yet developed. Much of it was land that still belonged to the Native Americans. Other parts were raw mountains, deserts, and open prairie.

The people on the west coast wanted to keep up with what was going on in the rest of the country. They had to wait weeks for news and letters to arrive if they were sent by wagons or carriages. They had to wait for months if the mail came by ships that had to sail all the way around South America!

OREGON

People were hungry for news, not least because the country was on the edge of a war between the slave-holding southern states and the northern states that had gotten rid of slavery. They needed to know what

was happening in business, and when to buy or sell their own goods. Just like today, having fresh information was very important!

FAST NEWS DELIVERY

Some men came up with a plan to deliver news to and from California that would take only ten days. It would involve fast horses and fast riders, with the riders changing from tired horse to fresh horse and then handing the mailbag to a fresh rider when they were tired themselves. The men figured that people who needed fast news would pay for the service.

U.S. DEPARTMENT OF THE INTERIOR
BUREAU OF LAND MANAGEMENT
PONY EXPRESS TRAIL
1860-1861

HOW IT WORKED

There was a telegraph system that connected the United States from the big cities like New York and Chicago to Missouri, on the Mississippi River. The men worked out a route across the prairies and the Rocky Mountains to the west coast. The route passed through what is now Kansas, Nebraska, Colorado, Wyoming, Utah, and Nevada before reaching California, a distance of over 1900 miles.

A single rider would start out either from Missouri or from Sacramento, California. The rider would have a fast horse, the minimum of supplies, and a bag of mail. The rider would go as fast as the horse could ride for ten or fifteen miles, until he came to the next relief station.

Pony Express Station

PONY EXPRESS R
For a brief 16 month period, d
and 1861, this was the Pony Exp
Mail was carried by horseback f
Missouri to Sacramento, California
days. The Pony Express ended in 18
HUMBOLDT National For
Pony Express Route

The Pony Express had almost 200 relief stations along the route the riders would take. Most of the stations were very primitive, but they had food, water, and—most important—fresh horses. The rider would race up to the station, jump off his horse, move his saddle and the mail bag over to the fresh horse, and be on his way again in about two minutes.

The relief station staff would take care of the tired horse, and prepare another fresh horse for the rider who would be coming from the other direction later in the day. Every hundred miles or so, a new rider would take over so the exhausted rider could have a rest and prepare to take another mail bag back in the direction he came from as soon as it showed up.

Pony Express Station

Pony Express Barn

The system could get a mail bag across the country in nine or ten days. The record was delivery of President Abraham Lincoln's first inaugural address, in less than eight days!

THE RIDERS

As you would expect, the riders were excellent horsemen. They had to move fast, and keep moving. They rode through rain and snow, over mountains and across rivers, and through areas where Native Americans were at war with the federal government.

Pony Express Statue

PONY EXPRESS

St. JOSEPH, MISSOURI to CALIFORNIA
in *10 days or less.*

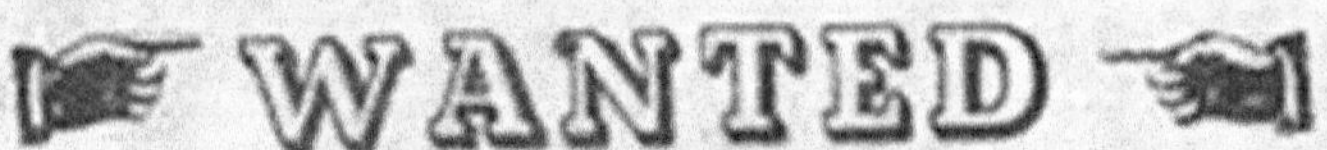

YOUNG, SKINNY, WIRY FELLOWS
not over eighteen. Must be expert
riders, willing to risk death daily.

Orphans preferred.
Wages $25 per week.

APPLY, **PONY EXPRESS STABLES**
St. JOSEPH, MISSOURI

The Pony Express hired young men, a lot of them teenagers, who had to weigh under 125 pounds. They got paid $100 a month, plus all the fast riding that any young man could want. At that time, the daily wage for unskilled labor would have been about $24 a month. It is said the company published advertisements saying "Orphans wanted!", and many young men without attachments responded to the challenge. There were no women Pony Express riders.

A SHORT-LIVED SERVICE

The Pony Express opened for business April 3, 1860, and had to close in October, 1861. Despite all the planning and all the hard work, it did not succeed.

Pony Express Stable
PONY EXPRESS STABLES

The start of the Civil War disrupted plans, and so did continuing fighting with Native American tribes along the route the riders had to take. But the biggest problem was this: by the end of 1861 there was a faster way to get messages to and from California.

On October 24, 1861, Western Union finished connecting the telegraph system in California with the main system in the eastern part of the country. Now messages could fly from coast to coast as fast as keyboard operators could tap them in! Two days later, the Pony Express closed its doors.

N.Y. TELEGRAPH
NEW YORK

SPEEDY PONY
EXPRESS FACTS

In the winter it took about twelve days to get a mail packet across the country. In the summer, it took less than ten days.

Pony Express Trail between Eagle Mountain and Fairfield Utah

KEEP OFF
THE PONY EXPRESS TRAIL
1860 - 1861

When the service started, the minimum cost, which would let you send a half-ounce letter, was $5. In 2015 dollars, that would be be over $125! At those prices, nobody was sending funny birthday cards to their relatives! Most of the mail was government documents and newspapers specially printed on thin, lightweight paper.

Despite the danger, extreme weather, and the possibility of accidents, only one Pony Express rider (and one mail sack) was lost while the service was active. As many as six riders died, but most of the mail sacks were recovered.

Pony Express National Historic Trail in Utah

The Pony Express used skinny kids as riders, not burly (and heavy!) cowboys. The riders were about the size of jockeys on a modern race course. Their average age was 20, but the company hired people as young as 14. The rules were different in those days about child labor and sending kids out into the wilderness to survive as best they could!

Riders had to promise not to swear, not to get drunk, and not to start fights. Things were dangerous enough without the riders starting their own trouble, though probably the riders did plenty of swearing when they were in tough spots.

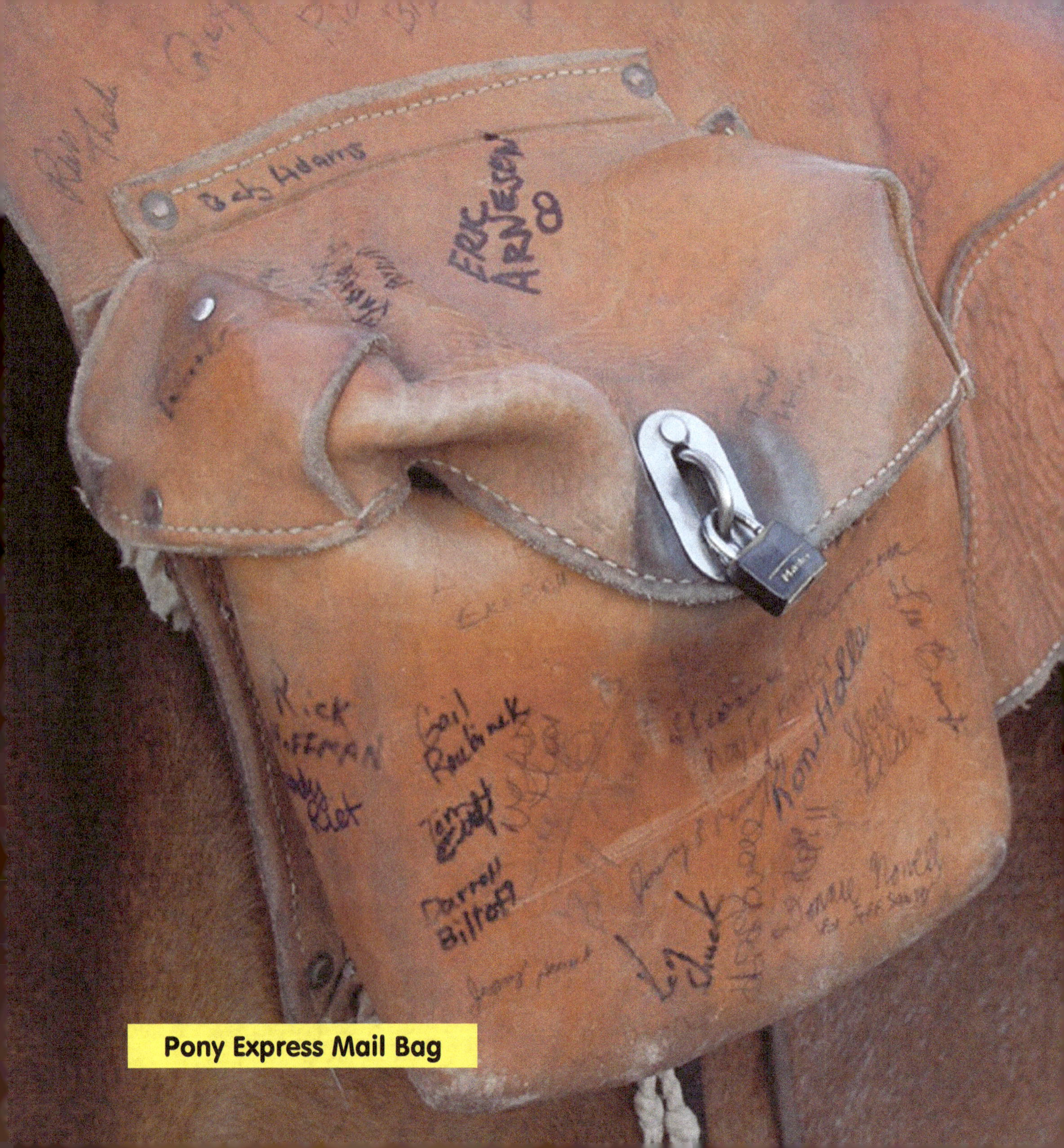

Pony Express Mail Bag

Each rider had a mail bag called a "mochila". It could hold twenty pounds of mail. The rider was also allowed about twenty pounds of equipment, including water, a horn he could blow to warn each station as he got near to it, and a weapon or two. At this time, the Paiute Nation was at war with United States settlers, and part of the route ran through the battle area.

The riders had the tough job of speeding along through dangerous conditions and all extremes of weather, but the people who ran the relief stations had a dangerous job, too. The stations were simple shacks with dirt floors, added to the side of the corrals for the horses. Many were in isolated areas, making them easy to attack. In 1860, Paiutes attacked and burned several stations and killed almost twenty of the station workers.

Pony Express Station

Ruby Valley Pony Express Station
ORIGINAL
PONY EXPRESS CA
ERECTED IN 1860 AT RUBY VALLEY STA
MOVED TO THIS SITE IN 1960
BY THE
NEVADA HISTORICAL

The Pony Express only operated for 19 months. During that time its 500 riders covered more than 500,000 miles on horseback and carried about 35,000 pieces of mail.

The U.S. Post Office issued a stamp to honor the Pony Express in 1869. It was the first stamp to celebrate an historic event instead of a person, such as a president.

UNITED STATES.
POSTAGE
TWO 2 CENTS

Robert Haslam aka Pony Bob

"Pony Bob" Haslam rode 380 miles in less than 40 hours in May, 1840, setting the Pony Express record. When he completed his first run going east from Friday's Station in Nevada, he found the next rider was afraid to take over because there had been Paiute warrior raids nearby.

Haslam decided to continue, and rode a total of 190 miles to Smith's Creek, where he delivered his mail sack to the rider waiting there. After a short rest, he took the west-bound mail sack and rode back to Friday's Station. He changed horses as planned, except at one relief station that had been burned by the Paiutes.

Gothenburg Pony Express Station

Pony Express National Historic Trail

Congress established the Pony Express National Historic Trail in 1992. Only in Utah and California can you see parts of the original Pony Express route as the riders would have seen it in 1860. The rest of the route is now covered with roads or is otherwise not available. But you can visit about 50 Pony Express relief stations, or the ruins of stations. That would be a fun trip!

There are many amazing stories from what we now know as the American West. Many of them involve the collision of Native Americans with settlers. Read Baby Professor books like What Happened Before, During, and After the Battle of the Little Bighorn?, The Wounded Knee Massacre, King Philip's War, and Getting to Know the Great Native American Tribes to learn more.

THE PONY
EXPRESS
1860
1861
SAN FRANCISCO
FRIDAY'S
SALT LAKE CITY
FT. LARAMIE
JULESBURG
FT. KEARNY
MARYSVILLE
ST. JOSEPH
ATCHISON
PONY EXPRESS TRAIL
THIS PLAQUE COMMEMORATES THE PASSAGE IN 1860 AND 1861 OF THE PONY EXPRESS RIDERS FROM SACRAMENTO TO SAN FRANCISCO THROUGH WHAT IS NOW ORINDA.
SPONSORED BY THE CITY OF ORINDA'S HISTORICAL LANDMARK COMMITTEE AND THE PONY EXPRESS TRAIL ASSOCIATION.

Visit

BABY PROFESSOR
EDUCATION KIDS

www.BabyProfessorBooks.com
to download Free Baby Professor eBooks
and view our catalog of new and exciting
Children's Books